W9-CRJ-835

4

*A People in Focus Book*

# THE EMPEROR GENERAL
## A BIOGRAPHY OF
# DOUGLAS MACARTHUR

## NORMAN H. FINKELSTEIN

**ᴅP** DILLON PRESS, INC.
Minneapolis, Minnesota 55415

To my parents, Mollie and Sydney Finkelstein, and
my wife's parents, Naomi and Irving Brandt

I wish to express appreciation to Lt. Col. Lyman Hammond, Jr., U.S. Army,
Ret. (director), Edward J. Boone, Jr. (archivist), and Jeffrey Acosta (assistant
archivist) of the MacArthur Memorial; the Brookline Foundation; the John F.
Kennedy Library Foundation; the Still Pictures Branch of the National Ar-
chives; William Riley, member of MacArthur's Honor Guard; and the United
States Military Academy Archives.

The author gratefully acknowledges permission to quote from the following
copyrighted material: *Reminiscences* by General of the Army Douglas MacArthur, McGraw-Hill Book Co., © 1964 by Time, Inc. All rights reserved.

**Library of Congress Cataloging-in-Publication Data**

Finkelstein, Norman H.
The emperor general.
(A People in focus book)
Bibliography: p.
Includes index.
Summary: Covers the life and career of the U.S. Army five-star
general from his early life in various military outposts to a career in
two World Wars.
1. MacArthur, Douglas, 1880-1964—Juvenile literature.   2. Gen-
erals—United States—Biography—Juvenile literature.   3. United
States. Army—Biography—Juvenileliterature.4.UnitedStates—His-
tory, Military—20th century—Juvenile literature. [1. Mac-
Arthur, Douglas, 1880-1964.   2. Generals]  I. Title.  II. Series.
E745.M3F56   1989      355'.0092'4  [B]  [92]   88-22863
                                                   CIP
ISBN 0-87518-396-4                                 AC

Dillon Press, Inc., 242 Portland Avenue South
Minneapolis, Minnesota  55415

Printed in the United States of America
1  2  3  4  5  6  7  8  9  10  98  97  96  95  94  93  92  91  90  89

# Contents

# Chapter/One

## Wild West Days

The official ticker tape parade down Broadway would begin at 11:00 A.M. on Friday, April 20, 1951. But the night before, an estimated one million people lined the route from New York's Idlewild Airport to the Waldorf Astoria Hotel in the heart of Manhattan. They stood and cheered as the guest of honor drove by. General of the Army Douglas MacArthur was home.

Earlier that day, the general had delivered a powerful speech to a joint session of Congress in Washington, D.C. Millions of people had listened to the historic address, and a short phrase from that speech was rapidly becoming the best-known quotation of the decade: "Old soldiers never die, they just fade away."

The public remembered MacArthur's successful direction of the campaign against Japan during World War II. The front page of the *Boston Evening Globe* for August 14, 1945, carried the dramatic news of the war's end with a gigantic headline: "President Truman Announces...JAPS SURRENDER...MacArthur to Accept Terms." Beneath the picture of the president of the United States was another of General MacArthur, supreme commander of Allied forces in the Pacific.

From 1945 to 1951, General Douglas MacArthur remained in the news. First he directed the occupation of Japan and helped Japan become a true democracy. Then, after the North Koreans invaded South Korea in 1950, he led the American and United Nations forces in Korea.

Douglas MacArthur was one of the few military leaders in American history to hold the rank of five-star General of the Army. He also held the largest number of medals ever awarded a member of any branch of the American military, including the highest decoration of all, the Medal of Honor.

These honors and decorations were earned during a period of army service that spanned the first half of the twentieth century. But MacArthur's relationship with the U.S. Army began even earlier— with his birth on January 26, 1880.

Douglas came from a line of famous MacArthurs, beginning with his ancestors from Scotland. His grandfather, Arthur MacArthur, was very active in the government and later became a Supreme Court Judge in Washington, D.C. Douglas's father, also named Arthur MacArthur, was very young when he decided on the army as his career. He became a hero in the Civil War and was awarded the Medal of Honor for his bravery in battle.

In 1875, the dashing army officer met a lovely southern belle at a Mardi Gras ball in New Orleans, Louisiana. Mary Pinkney Hardy—"Pinky" to her friends—was the twenty-two-year-old daughter of a well-to-do Virginia cotton merchant. A year later, Arthur and Pinky were married at Riveredge, the Hardy's mansion in Norfolk, Virginia.

Soon after the ceremony, Pinky found herself far removed from her southern life-style. Dutifully, she set up housekeeping in army fort after army fort in the remote parts of the western frontier.

The MacArthurs' first two children, Arthur III and Malcolm, were born back at the Norfolk mansion. Pinky wanted her children to at least enter the world surrounded by comfort and the warmth of a loving family. Douglas, however, was born in an army fort in Little Rock, Arkansas, before his mother could return to Riveredge.

Above: *The army barracks in Little Rock, Arkansas, where Douglas MacArthur was born.* Right: *Douglas (left) poses with his brother Arthur (right) in 1884.*

The early years of Douglas's childhood were spent in the wild territory of New Mexico. The army troops stationed at Fort Wingate protected settlers from attacks by American Indians and outlaws such as "Billy the Kid." The only contact with city life was the new railroad. Although the fort was a lonely place with few other children, Douglas found much delight in the adventure of the Wild West. Cavalrymen would sometimes stop in and tell the children tales of fierce battles with the Apache Indians.

Despite the cramped buildings and the rough life of the fort, Pinky MacArthur worked hard to

keep the family happy. She took her children on occasional visits to Riveredge in Virginia. On one of these trips, five-year-old Malcolm died of measles.

When Douglas was four years old, his father's Company K had to move by wagon and on foot to a new post at Fort Selden, near El Paso, Texas. Rumors of the fierce American Indian warrior Geronimo spread through the West, and the U.S. government wanted to add more reinforcements to the Texas-Mexico border. The MacArthurs were not eager to begin the 300-mile journey. However, young Douglas spent part of the trip marching at the head of the column alongside the first sergeant.

Once at the fort, the family did the best they could to settle in. In the three years that the MacArthurs lived at Fort Selden, Douglas and his brother Arthur lived the life that many children could only dream of. Douglas learned to ride and shoot, sat around campfires with grizzled soldiers, and watched his father drill the troops. He and his brother took long, bumpy rides on mule-pulled water wagons to the Rio Grande, the river that divided Texas and Mexico. Each evening the boys stood at attention with the soldiers as the bugle sounded and the flag was lowered.

Since Fort Wingate had no formal school,

*The MacArthur family at Fort Leavenworth, Kansas, in 1886.*

Douglas's mother took charge of the boys' education. Beyond the basics of reading and writing, she taught them a sense of loyalty and duty. "We were to do what was right no matter what the personal sacrifice might be," said Douglas. "Our country was to come first. Two things we must never do: never lie, never tattle."

When the news came that Company K would be transferred to Fort Leavenworth, Kansas, Douglas's parents were excited. This fort, an important army training center, would be a step upward for Douglas's father. For Douglas and Arthur, however, the new fort meant going to a real school. No

more riding ponies and shooting rabbits—now
Douglas would have to work.

Douglas missed his exciting life at Fort Selden,
and he was not a good student. When his father
was ordered to go to Oklahoma for a short time,
Douglas begged to go along just to get out of class.
His father simply pointed to Douglas's report card,
and Douglas remained in school.

The family wouldn't be in Kansas for long. In
1889, Arthur MacArthur was promoted to major,
after twenty-three years of army service, and was
assigned a new position in Washington, D.C. Now
there would be three generations of MacArthurs
in the nation's capital.

Living in the city of Washington was almost
too much for Douglas to bear. After growing up on
a horse, he was now surrounded by the ceremonies of government and politics. Even his school
seemed formal and stiff. At the Force Public
School, he had to wear a suit and tie every day.

In 1892, Douglas's brother Arthur received an
appointment to the U.S. Naval Academy at An-
napolis. After sixteen-year-old Arthur left for the
academy, Douglas didn't see much of him. His older brother, however, always set an example of success and ambition for Douglas to follow.

To Douglas's relief, his father was transferred

from Washington to Fort Sam Houston in Texas. Here, troops were called to patrol the banks of the Rio Grande for bandits and people who crossed the river without legal permission.

The move to Fort Sam Houston marked a turnaround in Douglas's attitude toward learning. At his new school, the West Texas Military Academy, Douglas took his studies seriously. In time, he won many school medals for his superior abilities.

The other cadets liked him, but since he was a day student and not a boarder, they didn't know him very well. In his third year at the academy, he became more popular as he began to take a more active role in the school. Although Douglas was never an outstanding athlete, he played football, baseball, and tennis.

In June 1897, when Douglas gave the commencement speech as the number-one student in his graduating class, his proud parents attended the ceremony. Douglas had come a long way from his struggling school years in Kansas and Washington, D.C.

# Chapter / Two

## *Mama's Boy*

By this time, Douglas was more than ready to get on with a military career. He and his parents decided that the U.S. Military Academy at West Point would be the best place for him to go after graduation. It was a competitive academy, however, and it would be tough for him to gain admission. Douglas's father and his grandfather asked many of their powerful friends to write letters of recommendation for Douglas.

Most candidates to West Point are appointed by members of the U.S. House of Representatives or the Senate. The MacArthurs tried to win a congressional appointment from Congressman Theabold Otjen, a long-time friend of Judge MacArthur's.

*Sixteen-year-old Douglas as a cadet at the West Point Military Academy.*

Douglas and his mother moved to Milwaukee, Wisconsin, so that they could establish Douglas as a resident of Otjen's district. His father did
not join them because he had received a promotion
to colonel and was given a post in Saint Paul,
Minnesota.

Once in Wisconsin, Pinky and Douglas settled
in at a hotel—the Plankinton House. There they
began to prepare Douglas for the West Point ad-
mittance exam. Although his grades at West Texas
Military Academy had been very good, he was still
weak in certain areas.

He registered for courses at Milwaukee's West
Side High School. Twice each day he trudged the
long distance between the hotel and his school. He
met regularly with private tutors and studied under
his mother's constant direction. Douglas had never
worked so hard in all his life.

During his stay at Plankinton House, he developed a strong friendship with the assistant desk
clerk there. They would talk about the future together. When the news of the Spanish-American
War reached Wisconsin, Douglas and his friend
were ready to join the army immediately. Douglas's
father talked them out of it.

In this war of 1898, the U.S. government tried
to help the Caribbean island of Cuba gain indepen-

dence from Spain. Douglas's older brother was in the navy at this time, and Douglas's father was promoted to major general, and appointed military governor of the Philippine Islands. In the end, the United States won Guam, Puerto Rico, and the Philippines from Spain, and Cuba gained its independence.

The day of Douglas's West Point examination finally arrived. Douglas, who had hardly slept the night before, was extremely nervous. His mother accompanied him to city hall, where the testing was, and offered him continual encouragement right up to the front door. "Be self-confident,. . . even if you don't make it, you will know that you have done your best. Now, go to it." All his long hours of hard work paid off. When scores were announced, Douglas MacArthur's name topped the list. He was on his way to West Point.

The West Point Douglas saw on June 13, 1899, was majestic. Overlooking the mighty Hudson River, the U.S. Military Academy projected an impressive image of strength and endurance with its castlelike buildings and beautiful landscaping.

While Douglas tackled the hard life of a new cadet, his mother made her home at the nearby Craney's Hotel. Also living at Craney's was the mother of Ulysses S. Grant III, the grandson of the former U.S. president. During the first year at West Point, both famous sons were teased by the other cadets for being "mama's boys."

In the summer of 1899, West Point had a tradition called hazing, in which older students teased and abused the new cadets. Douglas was targeted for "special attention" as the son of the famous General Arthur MacArthur, who was making headlines in the Philippines. Cadets made him recite his father's military record, or hang by his toes and fingers from a cot until he dropped to the floor. Douglas took the brutal treatment well.

In spite of that frightening start, West Point was like a dream come true for Douglas. At the academy, his grades were excellent. He studied hard, but was sometimes frustrated by the West Point teaching method of having students memorize rather than discuss daily assignments.

Once, in a physics class, the teacher asked Douglas to explain the theory of relativity. Douglas proceeded to recite words that he had memorized from the textbook.

"Do you understand the theory?" the teacher asked.

"No, sir!" Douglas said.

"Neither do I, Mister MacArthur," the smiling teacher responded.

*Douglas* (seated on the far right) *with other members of the West Point baseball team.*

Outside of their classwork, the cadets could participate in athletics. Douglas, as a member of the baseball team, played in the first baseball game between West Point and the naval academy. He was also the manager of the football team for one year.

Social life at the academy was limited to occasional dances and rare outings. Once in a while, the cadets could leave the gates to march in official parades or attend major sporting events as a group.

Douglas even needed permission to visit his mother at Craney's Hotel, but he often went to see her without it. Pinky MacArthur soon became popular with the West Point cadets. She usually had something special for her son and his friends to eat, and she also was good at watching out for officers when Douglas and his friends were "illegally" visiting with young women at the hotel. On one such visit in the hotel's back parlor, an officer came into the hotel. When Mrs. MacArthur ran to warn the cadets, they escaped through the cellar and made their getaway through the coal chute.

Because Douglas worked harder than he played, he ranked as the top student in his class for three out of his four years at West Point. Douglas's fellow students recognized his leadership skills. At the end of his third year, Douglas was named first captain of the Corps of Cadets—the highest honor West Point gives a student. For the next year, he would be the leader of all the West Point cadets. His four-year class average was one of West Point's highest ever.

On June 11, 1903, Douglas graduated from West Point, and received his commission as a second lieutenant in the U.S. Army. As he joined the "Long Grey Line" of West Point graduates, his mother and father sat proudly in the audience.

# Chapter/Three

## *Journey through the Far East*

Douglas spent the summer after his graduation on vacation in San Francisco, California, where his father was serving as commander of the U.S. Army Division of the Pacific. Douglas had the opportunity to watch his father "in action" with other military leaders. During the visit, Douglas tracked down and captured an escaped army prisoner. The surprised convict spat at MacArthur and yelled, "You damn West Pointers!"

Not long after his vacation, Second Lieutenant Douglas MacArthur was ordered to the Philippines. The United States was still in control of the islands, as a result of the Spanish-American War. Douglas was assigned to work on engineering jobs to strengthen defense positions.

Although this was his first visit to the Philippines, Douglas found a friendly welcome wherever he went. People remembered his father, and the MacArthur name was respected among natives and U.S. military staff. Douglas made friends with many Filipinos, including the young military leader, Manuel Quezon.

Also during this time, Douglas became very sick with malaria. He returned to the United States, where he was promoted to first lieutenant, and assigned to work with his father as the acting chief engineer of the Division of the Pacific.

The same year, Douglas's father was sent to Japan to observe and report on the Japanese military effort in the Russo-Japanese War. When the war was over, Arthur MacArthur undertook a special long-term mission throughout the Far East to survey military conditions in the region. He took his wife with him and requested the services of his son Douglas as his military aide.

Douglas joined his parents in Yokohama, Japan, on October 29, 1905, and three days later the family set out on its official journey. The tour lasted nine months. It was a time of quiet luxury, and travel was slow and elegant. Douglas and his parents visited military bases, dined with royalty, celebrated Christmas in Singapore, and viewed lifestyles totally alien to their own. From Japan to India, from Ceylon to Siam, they saw wondrous sights—the Khyber Pass, Shanghai, Hong Kong, Saigon, and Canton.

In Siam, Douglas was attending a formal dinner given by the king when the lights suddenly went out. Douglas had noticed the fuse box when he entered the room. He rose from his seat and changed the fuse. The king was so impressed that he offered the young lieutenant a military decoration.

As exciting as all this foreign travel was, Douglas and his father had important work to accomplish. Both MacArthurs observed the growing military and economic strength of Japan. They became even more sure that the Pacific was important for future U.S. military security.

Japan and the Philippines attracted the most attention from the travelers. Japan interested them because of its growing military strength and the way its people were devoted to their emperor. The MacArthurs studied the Philippines' development of a democracy like that of the United States.

When their long trip was over, the family returned to San Francisco. Arthur MacArthur's reports to Washington were well received. By an act of Congress, he was appointed to the special rank

*The MacArthur family in 1905. Back row: Douglas's brother Arthur; Arthur's wife, Mary; and Douglas. Front row: Douglas's mother, Pinky; Douglas's nephew, Arthur; and Douglas's father, Arthur.*

of lieutenant general, making him the highest-ranking officer in the United States Army. But the position he had always dreamed of—army chief of staff—escaped him. At the age of sixty-four, he retired from active service in disgust.

At the same time, Douglas's career was on the rise. In the fall of 1906, Lieutenant Douglas Mac-Arthur was assigned to study at the Engineer's School of Application in Washington, D.C. Douglas sometimes neglected his studies, however, because he had been assigned as an aide to President Theodore Roosevelt. Assisting at White House social events gave him the opportunity to meet political leaders and listen to their conversations.

Following the course at the Engineer's School, Douglas received an assignment in Wisconsin, close to where his parents lived. This closeness created problems with his commanding officer when Douglas began insisting on special favors and duty assignments to allow him more time with his parents.

For the next several years Douglas received assignments typically given to junior army officers, such as leading work details and drafting routine reports. His work was soon noticed by his superiors, and in February 1911, he was promoted to captain.

Shortly after his promotion, Douglas reported
for duty near the Texas-Mexico border. He took a
few hours off to visit the place where his military
career had been launched, the West Texas Military
Academy. He looked forward to this visit as a pleas-
ant way to relive the wonderful memories of his
happy student days. But Douglas had forgotten
how rude and coarse his fellow students had been
during his own years at the academy. The current
cadets proved to be no different, and their welcome of the new army captain was less than polite
and respectful. Glancing at his new army-issue hat,
the students laughed him off the campus by chant-
ing, "Where did you get that hat?" MacArthur
learned that beloved memories are sometimes best
left undisturbed.

In 1912, Douglas's father collapsed as he began
to deliver a speech to his old regiment. As he lay
dying, Arthur's friends knelt on the floor around
him and recited the Lord's Prayer. A former officer
ripped the flag from the wall and gently wrapped
it around him. "My whole world changed that
night," Douglas later said. "Never have I been able
to heal the wound in my heart."

After his father's death, Douglas's mother
came to live with her son. For a short time, they
occupied cramped quarters at Fort Leavenworth.

Then, Douglas was assigned to assist the Army General Staff, and they moved to Washington, D.C. The move meant a family reunion of sorts, since Douglas's brother Arthur, and his wife, Mary, were already living there.

Douglas was pleased with his new appointment on the General Staff. Although hundreds of other officers in the army outranked him, he was chosen to be one of thirty-eight officers in the army's top leadership group. The General Staff, including the chief of staff, Leonard Wood, soon learned to respect Douglas MacArthur's intelligence.

In 1914, the staff sent MacArthur to report on the U.S. Army's situation in Mexico. At that time, the United States was dangerously close to a war with Mexico. The Mexican general, Victoriano Huerta, had taken over the government just when Mexico seemed closer to a democracy. President Woodrow Wilson disliked Huerta and his new regime. At Veracruz, Mexico's main port, U.S. sailors and marines went ashore to occupy the city and to prevent a large German ship of ammunition from arriving. Veracruz was secured by the U.S. naval forces, at the cost of five hundred casualties (dead or wounded soldiers) on both sides.

MacArthur's job was to secretly scout the area, so that the U.S. Army could prepare for the possibility of an all-out war with Mexico. He took a dangerous and unofficial trip into the Mexican countryside to find locomotives to transport the troops. His report of the trip told just how dangerous it was: "At Salinas. . .we were halted by five armed men. . . .They opened fire. . . .in order to preserve our own lives I was obliged to fire upon them. Both went down. . ." Later in the journey, MacArthur faced more danger: "We were fired upon by three mounted men who kept up a running fight. . .one of these men passed the car. He sent one bullet through my shirt and two others that hit within six inches of me, forcing our return fire."

MacArthur was recommended for the Medal of Honor after this trip. He did not receive the medal because he had not been on an officially approved mission. However, upon his return to Washington, he was promoted to the rank of major and reappointed to the General Staff.

This short experience under fire was exciting. It could not, however, prepare MacArthur for the intense bloody fighting that lay ahead.

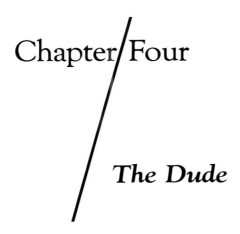

# Chapter/Four

## *The Dude*

World War I had already begun, although the United States would not enter the fighting until April 1917. Public opinion against Germany was growing steadily, but President Woodrow Wilson had a policy of strict neutrality—not taking sides—in the war.

During this period, Major Douglas MacArthur became military assistant to the new secretary of war, Newton D. Baker, and was the army's official spokesman to the press. He also actively debated with the General Staff about the use of National Guard troops in wartime.

The Guard was a civilian army that was controlled by state governments. Only in times of national emergency did the president control these troops. The General Staff finally declared that the National Guard would not be used to fight wars. But when the official document came around for MacArthur to sign, he added his comments that the president should have the option to use the Guard to supply a larger number of trained troops to the U.S. Army.

Shortly afterwards, MacArthur received a message to report to the secretary of war at once. Major MacArthur was ready to apologize and back down as a sign of loyalty to the rest of the General Staff. To his great surprise, Secretary Baker praised his stand and insisted that the National Guard option become the official army recommendation to the president.

With President Wilson's approval, the secretary of war could now begin assembling and training the Guard troops. MacArthur suggested creating a division of men from many states to symbolize the Guard's national purpose and downplay its regional character. Thus was born the famous Forty-second Division, called the Rainbow Division because its members came from all over the nation.

MacArthur also suggested appointing a strong officer from the General Staff to serve as the division's chief of staff. Without hesitation, Secretary

Baker turned to MacArthur and said, "It is you." Major MacArthur was flattered, but reminded Newton that only an officer with the rank of colonel could serve in that position. "You are now a colonel," said the secretary.

On April 6, 1917, the United States declared war on Germany and joined the Allies—France, Great Britain, and Russia. MacArthur had worked hard to build the Rainbow Division into a proud and effective unit. When officers at headquarters decided to split up the division, Colonel MacArthur was furious. He quickly turned to his friends at headquarters and in Washington, and the order was reversed. Though many resented MacArthur's actions, the Rainbow Division was saved.

While his division was still in training, Colonel MacArthur decided that he should scout out the enemy's troops. Without bothering to ask his superiors for permission, he attached himself to a French unit and traveled with them beyond enemy lines. The French were impressed, and General Georges de Bazelaire awarded him the French *croix de guerre*, or war cross. Not wanting to be outdone, the American army awarded MacArthur the Silver Star for heroism.

The terror of World War I shocked MacArthur's men. Heavy-duty artillery, poisonous gas,

*On an army maneuver in World War I, MacArthur looks over the troops.*

armored tanks, and the first combat airplanes led to a new kind of war. From one end of France to the other, soldiers on both sides dug honeycomb systems of ditches in the earth. The enemies faced each other and waged war from these foxholes.

Life in the trenches was nearly unbearable. In the summer, crawling insects invaded soldiers' clothes and equipment. In the winter, slushy ground made the men slip and slide. When it rained, slimy mud covered everyone and everything. The continuous stink was overpowering.

When the Rainbow Division set out on its first

attack, MacArthur led the scramble over the trench. With the shrill whistles of officers signaling the men forward, enemy fire ripped through the advancing line of soldiers. The Americans overtook the enemy position as MacArthur fought alongside his men.

Unlike many other officers, MacArthur was constantly visible to his men. They called him the Dude because of the attention he gave to his appearance.

MacArthur's military uniform was never totally according to regulation. He rarely wore a helmet, even in battle. Instead he wore a smashed-down officer's cap with the wire frame removed, which became his trademark. He liked to wear a turtleneck sweater with a large West Point A, and insisted on draping his neck with a four-foot scarf knitted by his mother. His trousers were always neat and pressed, and his boots, even in the worst weather, always seemed to be freshly shined. Most of the time, the only "weapon" he carried was a fancy riding crop—a foot-long rod.

The soldiers were not impressed by the clothes alone. What meant more to them was the brave leadership MacArthur demonstrated. Colonel Douglas MacArthur often accompanied his soldiers on even the most dangerous attacks.

On several occasions, MacArthur was felled by
poisonous gas. He received two Purple Hearts for
these injuries. If he had worn the required gas
mask, MacArthur probably would not have suffered these injuries (or received the medals). Since
he thought gas masks were ugly and undignified,
he never carried one.

Even though he would not use a gas mask and
wore a strange uniform, MacArthur was recognized
as a brave leader who had earned the love and
respect of his troops. On June 26, 1918, he was
promoted to the rank of brigadier general.

MacArthur's new command was the Eighty-
fourth Brigade of the Rainbow Division. To honor
his previous service as the Rainbow Division's
chief of staff, he was given a gold cigarette case
engraved "The bravest of the brave."

By mid-July of 1918, the German army
reached the outskirts of Paris. A German victory
would badly hurt the Allied cause. The Rainbow
Division fought bravely to defeat the Germans.
MacArthur led his men from one village to another
in constant hand-to-hand battle with the enemy
until they reached the Ourcq River. He was awarded two more Silver Stars for his leadership during
these important battles.

At the Ourcq River, MacArthur scouted enemy positions by himself. What he found made him suspect that the enemy was secretly pulling back its troops. He knew that a surprise attack would stop the Germans in their tracks. It was three-thirty in the morning, and MacArthur had not slept in four days, but he immediately ordered his men to "advance with audacity!" When the battle was over, American lines were finally secure, and the surprised Germans were on the run. MacArthur received the credit for this Allied victory. After a short rest, the action continued for MacArthur and his men as they bravely took part in the offensive, or attack, at St. Mihiel.

During the Meuse-Argonne offensive at Châtillon, MacArthur had not eaten for thirty-six hours when he spotted an old, shabby inn. He entered and eagerly requested food. The innkeeper responded with a five-course meal consisting of the only food available—potatoes. MacArthur feasted on potato soup, potato fricassee (stew), creamed potatoes, potato salad, and potato pie. Later, he commented that the meal had been the best he ever had.

With the Germans now on the defensive, capturing the Côte-de-Châtillon was the key to Allied success. Châtillon was a heavily armed outpost that defended against any American advance toward the

German border. MacArthur's commander, Major General Charles Summerall, ordered, "Give me Châtillon, MacArthur, or a list of 5,000 casualties."

"All right, General," MacArthur instantly responded, "we'll take it or my name will head the list."

On October 12, 1918, MacArthur began the attack. The Rainbow Division's losses were staggering. But after two solid days of fighting, the American victory was complete.

The hard-won victory at Châtillon almost marked the end of MacArthur's life. Because of a communications error, two other U.S. Army divisions suddenly overran the lines of the Forty-second Division. On his way to straighten out the mess, he was taken prisoner at gunpoint by a U.S. Army lieutenant. The lieutenant was sure that the strangely dressed general was a German officer! After a brief but embarrassing wait, the general was identified and released.

Brigadier General Douglas MacArthur was recommended for the Medal of Honor, America's highest military decoration, and for promotion to the rank of major general. His old boss, Secretary of War Newton Baker, endorsed the nomination by calling MacArthur "the greatest frontline general of the war."

On November 6, 1918, General John Pershing, the head of all Allied forces in Europe, appointed MacArthur commander of the entire Forty-second Division. On November 11, the war finally ended.

MacArthur's nomination for the Medal of Honor was denied, and the war ended before he could be promoted to major general. Instead, he was awarded a seventh Silver Star, a Distinguished Service Cross, and yet another Purple Heart.

On November 22, MacArthur, still a one-star general, regained command of the Eighty-fourth Brigade. They marched into Germany for a period of occupation duty, to help the conquered country adjust to Allied control.

In March 1919, General Pershing personally awarded MacArthur the Distinguished Service Medal. The "bravest of the brave" had become one of the most highly decorated American officers of World War I. As he headed home after eighteen months overseas, Douglas MacArthur could look forward to a bright future.

# Chapter/Five

## The Fruits
## of Victory

Upon his return to the United States, Douglas MacArthur was appointed superintendent of the United States Military Academy at West Point. For one who looked back with fondness on his own four years at the academy, this could have been a comfortable and enjoyable assignment. But MacArthur soon found that he had escaped the trenches of France only to face another battle—the fight to restore West Point to its earlier greatness.

During World War I, the immediate need for large numbers of trained officers had made it necessary to shorten the school's four-year course of study to one year. Time had damaged the academy in other ways. MacArthur quickly recognized that West Point's nineteenth-century teaching methods and courses did not work for the modern soldier.

Superintendent MacArthur began his duties on June 12, 1919. Using his new and powerful position, he set out to pull West Point into the twentieth century.

The academy's courses mostly covered military subjects and related areas such as engineering and mathematics. MacArthur updated the science courses and introduced classes in the liberal arts, such as history, government, and economics. He believed that an army officer had to be more than just a fighting man—he had to understand and be part of the world around him.

MacArthur's goal was to make each West Point graduate a leader of men. He ordered the cadets to attend established military camps where young officers-in-training would join regular army troops in real combat exercises under skilled officers. The superintendent thought that young sheltered cadets could "learn more of human nature, acquire understanding, sympathy and tact" by working with soldiers like those they would be commanding in a few years.

Thinking back to his own student experiences, MacArthur put an end to the harsh hazing. He also established a cadet honor code by which cadets were responsible for policing their own conduct.

Perhaps MacArthur's most lasting contribution to West Point was his physical education program. MacArthur believed that sports built a sense of common purpose and prepared young men, physically and mentally, for leadership.

MacArthur worked hard to get support to rebuild West Point. He made frequent trips to Washington, and he had special relationships with leaders of the army and members of Congress. But his efforts were not fully appreciated. While some faculty members applauded his work, others did not understand how he could tinker with West Point tradition. Alumni (former students) also criticized his changes.

When success was hard to achieve, the social aspects of MacArthur's job lightened his spirit. He and his mother had moved into the superintendent's house, and Pinky had become his official hostess. They entertained many distinguished people, including the Prince of Wales, the future king of England.

Although he usually liked to remain at home reviewing paperwork or reading a book, MacArthur sometimes attended fancy balls and elegant dinners. At one of these social occasions, Douglas met a beautiful, rich, and lively woman named Louise Cromwell Brooks.

On Valentine's Day, 1922, Douglas and Louise were married at the bride's family mansion in Palm Beach, Florida.

Pinky MacArthur was not pleased with her son's choice of bride, and she did not attend the wedding. The new Mrs. MacArthur had been divorced, and her name constantly appeared in the newspaper society columns. When Douglas and his wife returned to their West Point home, Pinky moved back to Washington, D.C., to live with her son Arthur's family.

The general and his bride did not remain at West Point for long. Just before the wedding, MacArthur had received an unexpected change in assignment. He was to go to the Philippines as commander of the Military District of Manila. In June, Douglas, Louise, and Louise's two children from a previous marriage set sail for Manila.

MacArthur was happy to see Manila again after an eighteen-year absence. His wife, however, missed her busy social life in America and was soon bored. She did not share her husband's fondness for his Filipino friends.

MacArthur's duties were not very exciting for him. He worked on surveys, military studies, and planning reports. He renewed friendships with Filipinos, many of whom later became leaders of their country. Since the U.S. government wanted to strengthen Philippine defenses in case there was a war, MacArthur helped organize and train Filipino soldiers.

Early in 1923, MacArthur's mother became seriously ill. The family hurried back to Washington. Pinky recovered, and the MacArthurs returned to Manila two months later. That same year, Douglas's brother Arthur, a highly decorated naval officer, died unexpectedly. This was a blow to Douglas, who had been quite close to his brother even though they didn't see much of each other.

MacArthur had been a one-star general for nearly five years. He was not the only one who felt it was time for a promotion. His wife and mother, in their own ways, were doing their best to help him advance by writing to important people in Washington. The women's efforts may or may not have helped, but in September 1924, Army Chief of Staff General Pershing announced MacArthur's promotion to major general. When the second star was pinned to his uniform January 17, 1925, forty-five-year-old Douglas MacArthur became the youngest major general in the U.S. Army.

The MacArthurs returned to the United States, and Douglas took command of the Army III

*MacArthur and his wife, Louise Cromwell Brooks MacArthur, arriving in the United States from the Philippines in 1925.*

Corps, based in Baltimore, Maryland. The family
moved into an estate near Baltimore that Louise
owned. Douglas's wife enjoyed the social life she
had missed in Manila, but he was not comfortable
in the country club setting. More and more, the
two went their own ways.

MacArthur soon settled into the routine daily
tasks of an army at peace. He made many speeches
and did public relations work.

In 1927, MacArthur had an unexpected opportunity. Just a few months before the Olympics, the
president of the U.S. Olympic Committee died suddenly. The committee needed a take-charge person
at once, and MacArthur's name was proposed immediately. His physical fitness and sports programs
at West Point were well known; in fact, they served
as models of excellence at many colleges and army
posts. Army Chief of Staff General Summerall
granted MacArthur a leave from the Army III
Corps to assume this position. MacArthur left for
the site of the 1928 Olympics—the Netherlands.

From the moment of his appointment up to
the final competition, Douglas MacArthur inspired
the members of the U.S. Olympic Team to do their
best. As he had at West Point, he participated in all
parts of their training, coaching, and preparations.
When the games were over, the United States had

*MacArthur* (back row, third from left), *is aboard the S. S. Roosevelt, on his way to the Olympic Games at Amsterdam, in the Netherlands.*

won twenty-four first-place medals and set a number of world and Olympic records.

Louise did not accompany Douglas to the Olympic games in the Netherlands. She had moved out of the Baltimore mansion and settled in New York.

When MacArthur went back to his army command, he was reassigned to Manila, this time as overall commander of the Department of the Philippines. "No assignment could have pleased me more," he wrote.

MacArthur returned to Manila without Louise. In June 1929, Louise divorced him.

In Manila, he spent time with his former Filipino friends, including Manuel Quezon, who was now a national political figure. For the most part, MacArthur spent his days in the Philippines quietly doing normal daily tasks.

On August 6, 1930, President Herbert Hoover appointed General Douglas MacArthur to serve as the army chief of staff. By right, the position of chief of staff, the army's highest post, should have gone to an older general with a higher rank. At fifty, MacArthur would be the youngest chief of staff ever. But he was also perhaps the most well-known officer in the U.S. Army. The *New York Times* described the appointment as follows: "General MacArthur has a faculty for doing the unexpected and he has the personality to get away with it. . ."

MacArthur was sworn into his new position on November 21, 1930, and was moved up to four-star rank. When MacArthur moved into the chief of staff's official quarters at Fort Myer, Virginia, his mother was with him. This was perhaps the proudest moment of Pinky's long life—Douglas had achieved the position his father had only dreamed of.

# Chapter/Six

## *Build Me a Son*

The stock market crash of 1929 had plunged the United States into economic disaster. Eight million Americans were out of work. Soup kitchens fed the hungry. The government in Washington, headed by President Hoover, seemed unable to deal with the situation.

The military faced difficulties, too. An antiwar mood gripped Congress and the country as national attention focused on problems at home. The army was half its normal size and was no longer receiving enough money to maintain its equipment.

Douglas MacArthur worked hard to strengthen and modernize the weakened army, but not because he liked war. "Every reasonable man knows that war is cruel and destructive," he said, "and yet

. . .history has proved that nations once great,
that neglected their national defense are dust and
ashes."

MacArthur fought a bitter battle with Congress. He argued that the country had to be prepared if war came. "I stormed, begged, ranted and
roared," he later wrote. The next war, he said,
would require the use of airplanes, submarines,
and tanks. The country needed to stockpile supplies and prepare industry to meet military needs at
a moment's notice. No one seemed to take MacArthur seriously. He felt that he alone knew what was
happening in the rest of the world.

Across two major oceans, political and military events provided warning signals of war. During 1931 and 1932, MacArthur made official trips
across the Atlantic to witness military preparations
in Europe. Adolf Hitler's Nazi party was already
gaining strength in Germany, and European countries were worried. In the Pacific, Japanese troops
invaded China and occupied Shanghai.

At home, antiwar feelings were stronger than
ever. Since the army still lacked money and political support, MacArthur worked on strengthening
the military organization from the inside. While he
worked to prepare the army for battles overseas, a
serious conflict grew in Washington.

In 1924, Congress had passed a bill granting World War I veterans (former soldiers) a one thousand-dollar bonus that would be paid in 1945. With the economic crisis of the Great Depression at its height in the early 1930s, many unemployed, homeless, and hungry veterans demanded their bonuses immediately.

In May 1932, thousands of veterans and their families traveled to Washington, D.C., to take part in the Bonus March. They held demonstrations and parades to force Congress to give them their money. Throughout the capital, they set up camps built of scrap lumber, tar paper, and tin. They called their camps Hoovervilles after their president, Herbert Hoover.

The Bonus Marchers continued their noisy demonstrations for almost two months while Congress debated their request. When a bill to grant them immediate payment failed, most of the marchers headed home. The thousands who remained, however, became involved in violent battles with police. When the Washington police could no longer control the situation, they appealed to President Hoover for help.

By three o'clock on July 28, 1932, General MacArthur had received an order from the secretary of war to "surround the affected area and clear

it without delay." The army troops met stone-throwing veterans, but they quickly brought the situation under control using tear gas. News photographers took pictures of unarmed, poorly dressed veterans—men who had fought for America—being chased by heavily armed combat troops on horseback.

Ignoring advice from his aide, Major Dwight Eisenhower, MacArthur decided to go into the streets to observe the action himself. MacArthur had arrived at work that morning dressed in a business suit. He quickly changed into the only uniform available and went out. In news photos, the chief of staff wearing a formal dress uniform with rows of ribbons and decorations seemed out of place on the tear-gas-filled streets. That image haunted MacArthur for years.

President Hoover and General MacArthur believed the Bonus March was a Communist attempt at revolution. They were sure that if the marchers had continued their protest, the government would have been in grave danger. The American public, however, sympathized with the veterans and blamed Hoover and MacArthur for what had happened.

Hoover lost the next election. The new president, Franklin D. Roosevelt, was sworn into office

*Douglas MacArthur at the Bonus March in Washington, D.C.*

on March 4, 1933. Leading the parade that day, on a beautiful white horse, was the army's chief of staff, General Douglas MacArthur.

Roosevelt needed to get America moving. Unemployment, poverty, and hunger were on the rise. Roosevelt began his presidency on an upbeat note. "We have nothing to fear but fear itself," he announced. The public, sensing his strong leadership, took heart. Although MacArthur felt closer to the politics of Hoover, he was soon involved in Roosevelt's New Deal.

Part of this program targeted the large number of unemployed young Americans. Roosevelt pushed a bill through Congress creating the Civilian Conservation Corps (CCC), which employed young men in government projects such as flood control and tree planting. But there was a problem. How could the government quickly organize, train, and transport 275,000 young workers?

Roosevelt turned to the army. To MacArthur's credit—and the army's pride—the job was done well. CCC recruits completed an army-run training course and were transported to U.S. Forest Service camps throughout the country.

Despite the army's success with the CCC program, Congress again cut the army's budget in 1934. MacArthur fought to save what he could.

When there was talk of laying off army staff to save money, he marched to Capitol Hill. When he finished presenting his arguments to Congress, enough money was restored to prevent the firings.

The budget cuts outraged the usually calm MacArthur. During one heated discussion in the Oval Office, he angrily raised his voice to the president. When Roosevelt roared, "You mustn't talk that way to the president!" MacArthur apologized and offered his immediate resignation. Roosevelt calmed down and dismissed the incident.

Secretary of the Army George Dern followed MacArthur outside. "You've saved the army," he told the general. But MacArthur did not feel much like a hero; after all the stress, he had just vomited on the White House steps!

MacArthur's four years as chief of staff were coming to an end. Amidst money battles and the Bonus March, he had strengthened the army and helped the soldiers feel confident. President Roosevelt decided to keep MacArthur on into a fifth year, until he could appoint a replacement.

MacArthur now faced a personal dilemma. As chief of staff, he held four-star rank; with the assignment over, any position he took in the army would be at a lower two-star rank.

His career problem was solved by the arrival of

an old friend, Manuel Quezon. Quezon, who would soon be the president-elect of the Philippine Commonwealth, made a special request of President Roosevelt. He asked Roosevelt to send MacArthur back to the Philippines as the commonwealth's military adviser to help the islands build up a defense force and prepare them for gaining independence as a nation.

This special position would allow MacArthur to remain an active officer in the U.S. Army. In addition, the Philippines would pay him an extra thirty-three thousand dollars each year.

When the ocean liner *President Hoover* sailed from San Francisco for the Far East in 1935, General MacArthur and his mother (now very old and sick) were on board. Major Dwight Eisenhower went along as MacArthur's chief assistant.

At a party on the ship, MacArthur met Jean Marie Faircloth. Jean was thirty-seven years old, unmarried, and on her way to meet friends in Shanghai. It was love at first sight. When the ship docked at Manila, Jean decided to stay there with Douglas instead of going on to Shanghai.

In December, Douglas's mother died. In life, she had almost always been there to guide him; in death, the lessons she taught remained constantly with him.

Douglas's home in Manila was a fancy air-conditioned apartment atop the Manila Hotel. Although he had a busy schedule, he managed to see Jean often. Their favorite pastime was going to the movies, which they did every night they could.

MacArthur did not like a showy social life. He was happiest among friends he had made in the Filipino community and in the Masons, a worldwide men's organization founded on religious, charitable, and moral principles. As a member of Manila Lodge No. 1, he made lifelong friendships with leaders of Philippine politics and business.

Most official business took place in his office. MacArthur impressed his visitors with his striking appearance and keen mind. He was more than fifty years old, but he looked and acted much younger. He stayed in good shape partly by walking—or rather, pacing—while talking or thinking.

MacArthur's job was to prepare the Filipinos to defend themselves. He insisted that the best way for the Filipinos to defend the islands was to prevent any enemy from landing troops on the beaches and gaining a foothold.

Large numbers of Filipino soldiers had been through basic training, but they still needed uniforms, equipment, and arms. MacArthur also saw the need for an officer corps and set about establishing a military academy like West Point. However, as soon as he began vigorously planning and organizing, his old enemy—the army budget—reappeared.

MacArthur lacked money, but he did not lack showmanship. On October 24, 1936, he was sworn in as field marshal of the Philippine Armed Forces. He took the oath dressed in a fancy uniform he had designed himself. Many Americans thought he looked ridiculous, but the Filipinos were impressed.

In early 1937, MacArthur accompanied President Quezon to Washington, where they both tried to convince American leaders to provide weapons and money for the Philippine military. Congress was not willing.

MacArthur did manage to make the trip personally satisfying. First, he had his mother's body buried next to his father's in Arlington National Cemetery. Second, he married Jean Faircloth—"the smartest thing I have ever done," he later said.

The ceremony took place on April 30, 1937, at the New York City Municipal Building. Only a few friends were present. Then, while Quezon continued on a world tour, Douglas and Jean returned to Manila.

On February 21, 1938, the MacArthurs' only

child was born. Since Jean and Douglas were busy with official duties, they hired a Chinese woman to help care for the child. Loh Chiu (as a small joke, they called her Ah Cheu), became a member of their family.

Arthur MacArthur IV quickly became the center of his father's life. Friends could not help but notice the change in the proud father. The general, who appeared stern and formal in public, sat down on the floor to play with his son. There was nothing the adoring father would not do for Arthur, whom he nicknamed Sergeant.

Each morning, little Arthur entered his father's bedroom with his constant companion, a stuffed rabbit named Old Friend. Together, father, son, and rabbit marched around the room while General Douglas MacArthur yelled, "Boom! Boom!"

When Arthur was very young and the family was still in the Philippines, the general sat down one evening and wrote a prayer:

### Build Me a Son

Build me a son, O Lord, who will be strong enough to know when he is weak, and brave enough to face himself when he is afraid; one who will be proud and unbending in honest defeat, and humble and gentle in victory.

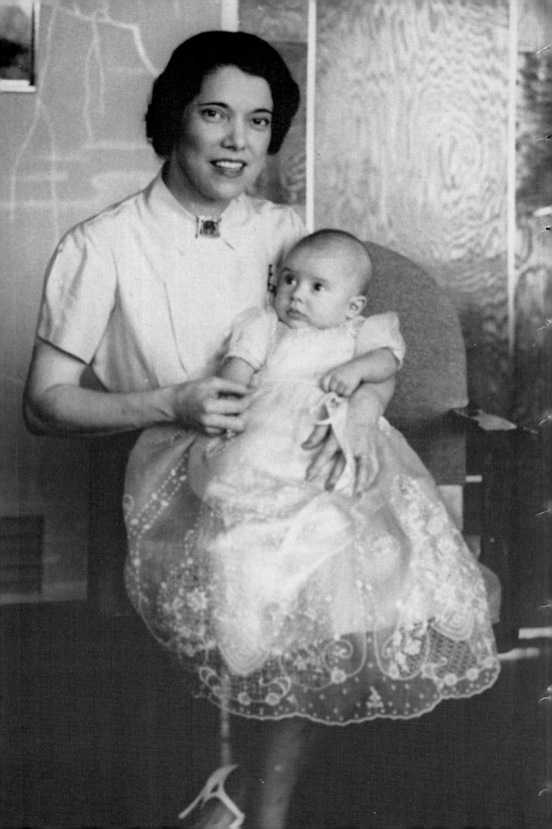

Build me a son whose wishes will not take the place of deeds; a son who will know Thee— and that to know himself is the foundation stone of knowledge.

Lead him, I pray, not in the path of ease and comfort, but under the stress and spur of difficulties and challenge. Here let him learn to stand up in the storm; here let him learn compassion for those who fail.

Build me a son whose heart will be clear, whose goal will be high, a son who will master himself before he seeks to master other men, one who will reach into the future, and never forget the past.

And after all these things are his, add, I pray enough of a sense of humor, so that he may always be serious, yet never take himself too seriously. Give him humility, so that he may always remember the simplicity of true greatness, the open mind of true wisdom, and the meekness of true strength.

Then I, his father, will dare to whisper, "I have not lived in vain."

(Courtesy MacArthur Memorial)

*Jean MacArthur holds little Arthur IV, in 1938.*

# Chapter/Seven

## *I Shall Return*

MacArthur's professional life was not as quiet as his family life during those years. In August 1937, he had received disturbing news. The army was ending his tour of duty in the Philippines and ordering him home. Since he saw no other suitable place for himself in the army, MacArthur had submitted his resignation. Expressing "deep regret," President Roosevelt accepted his decision.

To mark the end of his thirty-eight years of service, MacArthur would retire as a full general (four stars), the rank he had held as chief of staff. The general was expected to return to Milwaukee, the city of his father and grandfather, and "devote his time to cultural activities." But Douglas MacArthur was not quite ready to "just fade away."

President Quezon felt that he and his friend MacArthur had been betrayed. Quezon invited his friend to continue as his own military adviser. MacArthur's job would be the same, with one important difference: from now on, MacArthur would not represent the United States. MacArthur accepted Quezon's offer.

Many Filipino leaders, including President Quezon, did not believe their country could defend itself in a war. Although Philippine leaders respected MacArthur, they ignored his warnings to build up their own army.

Soon, however, the United States began to realize the seriousness of the Japanese threat. On July 26, 1941, MacArthur was called back into active duty as commanding general of the United States Army forces in the Far East. Supplies began arriving by the shipload. Huge B-17 bombers and modern fighters, which MacArthur knew were needed to defend the Philippines, arrived from Hawaii. Finally, with increasing Japanese naval and air activity in the area, U.S. forces in the Pacific went on full alert, ready for war.

While Japanese representatives talked to U.S. leaders in Washington, MacArthur prepared for attack. He ordered troops to get ready to defend the beaches. Their mission was to dig in and fight at the shore to prevent the enemy from landing on Philippine soil. This plan was doomed from the start. The Philippine shoreline was vast, and there were not enough well-trained troops to cover it.

At eight o'clock on Sunday morning, December 7, 1941, airplanes took off from Japanese carrier ships and attacked the U.S. naval fleet at Pearl Harbor, Hawaii. Within moments, a radio message flashed in the Philippines: "Air raid on Pearl Harbor. This is no drill." The United States was at war with the empire of Japan.

In short order, the Japanese attacked Hong Kong, Thailand, Guam, and Wake Island. On December 8, 1941, Japanese bombers reached the Philippines. In a surprise attack on Clark Field, they practically destroyed MacArthur's newly arrived air force.

The initial success of the Japanese quickly broke MacArthur's basic plan to hold them off at the beaches. The poorly trained and poorly equipped Filipino forces crumbled. Many Filipinos joined armed guerrilla groups (independent fighting groups) in the mountains; others just disappeared into the countryside. Before long, MacArthur realized that he could not save Manila.

On December 24, the Philippine government and the American military command moved over

# The Far East in World War II

to the Rock—the island of Corregidor. There, at
the mouth of Manila Bay, a bomb-proof tunnel
had been built deep inside a mountain. The Malinta Tunnel had its own electrical and air supplies,
hospital, storage, and shops, and it could survive
almost any type of enemy attack.

Within the tunnel, MacArthur and Quezon set
up headquarters. Their hope was to hold out until
the United States could send supplies and fresh
troops.

But that help never came. With Japan in near
total control of the sea, U.S. ships could not get
through, although submarines managed to bring in
some supplies. On January 2, 1942, Japan's General Homma and troops of the Japanese Imperial
Army entered Manila.

Jean and little Arthur had also moved into the
Malinta Tunnel. Like the general, they constantly
displayed a courageous spirit that others noticed
and admired. Mrs. MacArthur took care of the
sick and wounded while her four-year-old son
played under the watchful eyes of Ah Cheu.

MacArthur displayed the same coolness under
fire he had shown during the First World War. As
bombs fell, he casually stood outside the tunnel to
observe the Japanese air attacks that were slowly
destroying the Rock. The soldiers on Corregidor,

*Four-star General MacArthur in the Philippines with his corn-cob pipe.*

who were used to seeing the general, admired his bravery.

The men on Bataan (a peninsula on the west side of Manila Bay) developed a different opinion of MacArthur. They called their commander Dugout Doug because he was hardly ever seen on Bataan, where most of the American troops were.

MacArthur did make a torpedo boat crossing to Bataan on January 10. He told the men that supplies were ample and that help was on the way. When the sick and hungry men on Bataan realized that MacArthur had been wrong, his reputation fell even more.

With no hope for additional troops, fresh supplies, food, and medicine, the end was near for the brave fighters on Bataan and Corregidor. President and Mrs. Quezon escaped to safety on the last submarine trip from the island.

MacArthur was asked to leave Corregidor. The general refused—he could not leave his men at this important time. On February 22, 1942, however, MacArthur received a direct order from President Roosevelt to leave the Philippines and go to Melbourne, Australia. There he would take command of American forces in the Pacific and plan the war against Japan.

MacArthur faced a court-martial if he stayed,

and cries of desertion if he left. He thought hard about what he should do. Finally, he decided that he had no choice but to honor President Roosevelt's orders. He arranged for an orderly transfer of power and appointed General Jonathan Wainwright commander of all U.S. troops in the Philippines.

Other details also had to be arranged. MacArthur's family, Ah Cheu, and the staff he needed to establish a new command in Australia would accompany him. The party would leave Corregidor by boat and make its way through Japanese-controlled waters to the Philippine island of Mindanao. If they made it that far, they would transfer to aircraft for the trip to Australia.

On the evening of March 11, 1942, the passengers boarded four small, wood-hulled PT (patrol torpedo) boats for the dangerous trip. Each passenger was allowed one suitcase. Little Arthur carried his stuffed rabbit on board. While American guns fired at Japanese positions on the mainland, the boats set out to sea.

For nearly two days, the boats cut through continual sea spray, rocking and tossing their seasick passengers. At times, those on board were sure they would not make it—if a Japanese plane spotted them, or if a shore station caught sight of them, or if they ran into an enemy ship, it would be all over. Finally, they sighted Mindanao.

On Mindanao, the MacArthur party was driven to the Del Monte pineapple plantation. There they waited through four days of Japanese air raids for the plane to Australia.

The airplane ride was just as uncomfortable as the PT boat ride had been, but at least it was dry. The travelers were headed for Darwin, Australia. However, Japanese planes picked just this time to raid Darwin, and the MacArthurs were sent instead to an emergency field fifty miles away. By the time they landed, the passengers were totally exhausted.

Before MacArthur and his party could even begin to relax, Japanese bombers were spotted heading their way. The group was hurried onto yet another plane for a four-hour ride to Alice Springs.

A special train was sent to bring the MacArthur party to Melbourne. When MacArthur's train pulled into Adelaide on the way to Melbourne, reporters were waiting. MacArthur briefly explained that President Roosevelt had ordered him to Australia to lead the fight against Japan. Then, in a message to the Philippine people, MacArthur spoke his most famous words of the war: "I came through and I shall return."

For MacArthur, his time away from the Philip-

pines would be long. For the men he had left behind on Bataan and Corregidor, the time was
marked by death and torture. Hungry, weakened,
and diseased, they finally surrendered and were
marched off to prisoner-of-war camps. The Japanese were so brutal and cruel that this trip became
known as the Bataan Death March. Thousands of
American and Filipino soldiers died before they
could reach camp. The Japanese were soon in total
control of the Philippines.

Meanwhile, news of MacArthur's safe arrival
in Australia reached the West. America went wild.
Over the next few weeks, newspapers and maga-
zines carried stories about MacArthur. Because of
his brave stand on Corregidor and his dramatic sea
escape, he was considered a national hero. People
named streets, bridges, buildings, and babies after
him. The National Father's Day Committee chose
him as the Number One Father of 1942.

On March 26, 1942, President Roosevelt
awarded Douglas MacArthur the Medal of Honor.
Douglas and Arthur MacArthur are the only father
and son both to have received this medal.

# Chapter/Eight

## *I Have Returned*

The United States, China, Great Britain, Canada, France, the Soviet Union, Australia, and several smaller countries joined together as the Allied powers. The Australians and General MacArthur agreed that the Allies needed to pay more attention to the Pacific war. The Joint Chiefs of Staff in Washington also agreed and set up two Pacific commands.

One, called the Southwest Pacific Area, including Australia, they gave to MacArthur. The other, called the Pacific Ocean Areas, they gave to Admiral Chester Nimitz. In short order, convoys of ships carrying hundreds of thousands of American troops headed toward Australia and the Pacific.

MacArthur's first objective was to make sure

Australia was completely safe. Early in the war, American intelligence services had found out how to read Japan's military codes. Through these codes, MacArthur had advance warning that the Japanese were planning a surprise sea attack on Port Moresby, New Guinea, only one hundred miles from Australia. He and the Allies were able to prepare for the attack.

The Battle of the Coral Sea, as it was called, took place in April 1942, and was fought mainly by carrier-based aircraft. Despite great losses in ships and pilots, the Japanese continued to pursue the attack of Port Moresby. They next attempted a land invasion from their base at Buna.

After months of no-win battles, MacArthur finally had enough. In December 1942, he appointed a tough new commander, Lieutenant General Robert Eichelberger. MacArthur ordered him, "Take Buna or don't come back alive!" Eichelberger's soldiers drove the Japanese from Buna by mid-January.

MacArthur visited New Guinea for long periods to observe the battle scene. He was not pleased with the air corps, so he appointed General George Kenney to take command. Kenney immediately began to improve the air force. As MacArthur had predicted, American pilots began to experience victories on land and sea. The front grew, and the air force constantly needed new landing fields from which to launch attacks. MacArthur quickly provided them.

In early August 1942, a large American force had landed on Guadalcanal. Both sides suffered heavy casualties in six months of fierce fighting through swamps and jungles. For Americans, this was a new kind of war. The Japanese were experienced jungle fighters, totally devoted to victory for the emperor. They did not believe in surrender. If they were surrounded and outnumbered with no chance of escape, most Japanese soldiers would either kill themselves or try a final attack on the Americans.

In early 1943, MacArthur had perfected an attack plan that allowed Allies to advance toward Japan with as little loss of life as possible. He had American troops work their way toward Rabaul, New Guinea, from two directions. Admiral William Halsey approached on one side along the Solomon Islands, while MacArthur advanced up the New Guinea coast. The experienced Japanese troops on Rabaul waited for the attack. To their astonishment, the Americans never came!

MacArthur simply bombed Rabaul by air and proceeded to capture other, weaker Japanese positions. U.S. naval forces then cut Rabaul off from Japanese shipping. For the rest of the war, Japanese troops on Rabaul were useless.

MacArthur used the same plan at other strong Japanese bases in the Pacific, with equal success. He called this tactic leapfrogging; "Hit 'em where they ain't" became an American motto.

Throughout the war, MacArthur commanded at least eighty landings of troops in the Pacific. Amazingly, fewer than thirty thousand Allied soldiers among MacArthur's troops died. No other general in World War II captured as much territory with so little loss of life.

As the war continued, frontline soldiers were surprised to find their four-star general right there with them under fire on a shell-littered beach. True to form, MacArthur was never dressed for battle— no helmet and no battle gear, only his fancy, gold-braided officer's cap and a corncob pipe. His familiar figure gave courage to the troops.

MacArthur often angered his troops, however. Sometimes his overconfidence would backfire. In the midst of a raging battle, he would have public relations people issue news releases announcing an Allied victory. While the readers of American and Australian newspapers were filled with appreciation, soldiers were still being killed or wounded.

*General MacArthur goes ashore in landing craft as his forces fight and capture Japanese-held Pacific islands.*

MacArthur displayed a keen sense of drama in nearly everything he said or did. For one thing, he referred to himself in third person, as in "MacArthur wishes it to be known that. . ." This habit irritated some people, but it all added to his dramatic flair.

In letters home to his wife, General Eichelberger referred to MacArthur as Sarah, after a famous actress. Years later, Dwight Eisenhower spoke of the time he spent "studying dramatics" under MacArthur.

In many ways, MacArthur was an old-fashioned man who loved honors and ceremonies. He insisted on using symbols of rank and authority. Rumors of MacArthur's fancy living spread throughout the Pacific. In Australia, highly visible bodyguards and escorts surrounded him as he sped from home to office. His sleek, black automobile carried four stars in the front and the license plate USA-1 in the rear. Jean's car was USA-2. At Port Moresby, and later at Hollandia, he lived in buildings that the insect-infested infantry saw as palaces.

MacArthur continuously complained about the lack of support he received from Washington and London. With some reason, he felt that Allied leaders placed more effort on the war in Europe than on the one in the Pacific. Allied forces in the

Pacific were making progress, and decisions had to
be made. What route should they take to the Japanese home islands? Who should lead the attack?

The Joint Chiefs of Staff wanted to capture
Formosa (a Japanese-occupied island off the coast
of China), and use it as a base from which to attack
Japan. MacArthur wanted to use the Philippines as
a stepping-stone to Japan. He argued that Formosa
would take more time to win and cost many more
lives. Even more important was America's close
relationship to the Philippines and its people.

After several meetings at which the navy described its plans to the president, MacArthur
clearly presented his own. When the discussions
were over, Roosevelt decided that MacArthur
should, after all, retake the Philippines. From there,
the Allies would move on to Okinawa at the door-
step of Japan.

But first, MacArthur had to capture more island bases north of Australia from which he could
launch American planes and ships toward the Philippines. The general was aboard the *Nashville* as his
troops landed on one of those islands, Morotai.
Shortly after the soldiers stormed ashore, MacArthur wandered about the beach checking details.
They were only three hundred miles from the Philippines. MacArthur gazed across the water and

murmured, "They are waiting for me there. It has been a long time."

By mid-October, the largest naval fleet ever assembled—well over eight hundred ships—stood silently off the coast of the Philippine island, Leyte. Early on the morning of October 20, 1944, big guns on the mighty warships boomed into action. The first Americans began landing on Leyte beaches a few hours later. Japanese opposition was light.

At one o'clock that afternoon, MacArthur and Sergio Osmena, the new president-in-exile of the Philippines (Manuel Quezon had died in August), headed toward the beach in small boats. When the boats were unable to proceed because the water was too shallow, MacArthur and his party waded ashore.

MacArthur spoke into a microphone, delivering a short speech to the people who had long awaited him: "People of the Philippines, I have returned! By the grace of Almighty God, our forces stand again on Philippine soil. . . .Rally to me."

After MacArthur's departure in 1942, the guerrilla movement in the Philippines had grown stronger. The freedom fighters, who came from almost all political, social, and religious communities, shared the belief that MacArthur would keep his word. "I shall return!" became their slogan; it

*MacArthur wades ashore at Leyte in the Philippines in 1944.*

was painted on walls, and it appeared on cigarette packages brought along with guns and ammunition by daring U.S. submarine crews. These fighters had bravely harassed the enemy on their own. Now they were prepared to join American forces in a final campaign to drive the Japanese from the Philippines.

The fight would not be easy. The Japanese did not want to lose the valuable Philippine Islands. Gathering their shrinking fleet together, the Japanese made an unsuccessful attempt to turn the Americans back at the Battle of Leyte Gulf. The Japanese were so desperate that they trained kamikaze (suicide) pilots to fly their planes directly into American ships, killing themselves in the attacks.

On December 16, 1944, President Roosevelt announced the promotion of four army generals and three navy admirals to five-star rank. General Douglas MacArthur and his former aide, Dwight Eisenhower, would hold the new rank of General of the Army.

With General of the Army MacArthur in command, the invasion of Luzon in the northern Philippines took place in January 1945. By February 3, the first American troops entered Manila. Fighting was fierce as American and Japanese troops engaged in hand-to-hand combat. It took a month to defeat the Japanese. The losses were high, and the city was virtually destroyed.

Fighting throughout the Philippines would last to the very end of the war. However, on February 27, 1945, in a ceremony at Malacanan Palace in Manila, the commonwealth government of the Philippines was formally returned to office. The Filipinos could not thank MacArthur enough. The Philippine Congress declared him an honorary citizen of the Philippines. Postage stamps and coins were issued with his likeness and the title Defender-Liberator.

When the American and Filipino prisoners of

*General MacArthur inspects Corregidor after its recapture from the Japanese in 1945.*

war were finally free, MacArthur visited them to offer comfort. In a moving ceremony on Corregidor, after a fierce battle that took many Japanese and American lives, MacArthur ordered the American flag raised again over his former headquarters. "Have your troops hoist the colors to its peak and let no enemy ever haul them down," he proclaimed.

MacArthur established new headquarters in Manila. With the danger of fighting over, his wife and son left Australia by ship and returned to the Philippines in March.

On April 12, 1945, President Franklin D. Roosevelt died. MacArthur and Roosevelt had disagreed on many policy discussions, but they had respected one another. Now MacArthur would have to deal with a president he did not know, Harry S. Truman.

He would also have to deal with more and more complex military problems. While fierce battles raged throughout the Pacific, American planes increased their near-daily raids upon Japan, causing terrible damage. Japan's largest and most important cities were destroyed by the bombings. The Japanese lost hope, and their emperor, Hirohito, looked for a way to end the war. Meanwhile, MacArthur and others made detailed plans for the Allied invasion of Japan.

Before launching their full-scale attack, the Allied governments presented Japan with an opportunity to end the war. The Potsdam Declaration laid down certain requirements under which the Allies would accept a surrender. Japanese government leaders debated the document, but reached no conclusions. They did not realize that the decision was about to be made for them in a horrible way.

U.S. scientists had been working to create the atom bomb—the most powerful and terrible wea-

pon of destruction ever invented. During the international conference at Potsdam, Germany, President Truman received the word that the atom
bomb had been tested successfully in Alamogordo,
New Mexico. For Truman the bomb meant one
thing—a quick Japanese surrender. He and his advisers believed that millions of lives could be saved
if the bomb could end the war. If the United States
did not use this new weapon, Allied forces would
have to launch a large-scale invasion of Japan.

The U.S. government gave a general warning
to Japan, without mentioning the bomb. Japan did
not give up.

On August 6, 1945, the first atom bomb was
dropped on the Japanese city of Hiroshima. Although seventy thousand people were killed in the
explosion, Japan still did not surrender. Three days
later, a second bomb was dropped on Nagasaki—
killing thirty thousand people and forcing Japan's
final surrender.

The Japanese requested only that the position
of emperor must remain. To the Japanese people,
the emperor was more than just the country's
ruler; he was the symbol and spirit of the nation.

The Japanese government formally accepted
the Allied terms of surrender on August 15.
Throughout the United States, joyful citizens cele-

brated V-J (Victory over Japan) Day as a national holiday. The war in Europe had ended on May 7. The killing was over, and the world could turn its attention to peace.

President Truman appointed General of the Army Douglas MacArthur as supreme commander for the Allied forces. He ordered MacArthur to go to Japan to accept the official surrender of the Japanese empire.

On August 28, American units came to Japan to make arrangements for MacArthur's arrival. The soldiers felt nervous as they landed at the Atsugi airfield just outside Yokohama. They had every right to be nervous; some Japanese were unwilling to accept the emperor's radio announcement of the surrender. Yet, the Americans were received with politeness and warmth.

On August 30, MacArthur's personal C-54 plane, *Bataan*, touched down at Atsugi. As he walked, unarmed, down the steps and onto the field, his aides held their breath. Later, Winston Churchill, the prime minister of England, remarked that MacArthur's unarmed landing at Atsugi was the bravest event of the entire war.

The Japanese were gracious. As the official cars made their way to the New Grand Hotel in Yokohama, thirty thousand Japanese troops, with rifles in their hands, lined the route. The presence of so many armed enemy troops caused concern. The Americans were particularly puzzled that the troops faced away from the motorcade. Later this was explained as a sign of honor; ordinary Japanese were not permitted to gaze upon the emperor, and MacArthur was being shown the same respect.

At dinner in the hotel dining room, the general was served a delicious-looking steak. His aide was afraid the meat had been poisoned and wanted a Japanese to taste a piece first. MacArthur only laughed, raised a forkful of steak to his mouth, and said dramatically, "No one can live forever."

On September 2, 1945, the U.S.S. *Missouri* sat calmly in Yokohama Harbor in the Tokyo Bay, surrounded by hundreds of other U.S. Navy ships. Both sides gathered on deck to sign the official document. As American sailors hung over the rails to catch a view, the final drama of the war took place. On one side, dressed in formal wear and ill-fitting uniforms, were the defeated Japanese leaders. On the other side, near a microphone from which General MacArthur would speak, were the official representatives of the Allied countries who had been at war with Japan.

The ceremony opened with a prayer and the "Star Spangled Banner." Then MacArthur ap-

*On board the* Missouri, *MacArthur signs the Japanese surrender document. Directly behind MacArthur is General Jonathan Wainwright.*

proached the microphone. Standing behind him was General Jonathan Wainwright, recently freed from years in a Japanese prisoner-of-war camp. MacArthur spoke:

> We are gathered here, representatives of the major warring powers, to conclude a solemn agreement whereby peace may be restored. . . .It is my earnest hope and indeed the hope of all mankind that from this solemn occasion a better world shall emerge out of the blood and carnage of the past—a world founded upon faith and understanding—a world dedicated to the dignity of

man and the fulfillment of his most cherished
wish—for freedom, tolerance and justice.

The signing began. MacArthur signed last and
used several pens as he signed, giving one to General Wainwright and saving another for his son,
Arthur. At 9:25 A.M. the general rose and declared,
"These proceedings are now closed."

A few moments later, MacArthur returned to
the microphone to deliver a message of hope to the
American people. His words showed that while he
was a man of war by training and profession, he
was also a man of peace: "Today the guns are silent.
A great tragedy has ended. . . . We must go forward
to preserve in peace what we won in war."

# Chapter/Nine

## *The Emperor of Japan*

Within a week after the Japanese surrendered, Mac-Arthur had established himself in Tokyo. His family's new home had served as the American embassy before the war. When the general inspected this fancy building, he found the inside in terrible condition. He also found a picture of George Washington still hanging on one wall. Turning toward the image of the first president, MacArthur saluted and said, "General, it's been a long time but we finally made it."

The general's office and headquarters were in the Dai Ichi (Number One) Building, directly opposite the emperor's palace in the center of the city. From this location, he governed Japan between 1945 and 1951, according to orders issued by President Truman: "From the moment of surrender, the authority of the Emperor and Japanese Government to rule the state will be subject to you." In the history of the United States, never was such power given to one person.

As the Allied occupation began, neither the Americans nor the Japanese knew what to expect. Winners of a war sometimes treat the losers quite badly. The Japanese expected to be overrun by soldiers seeking revenge; they were pleasantly surprised by the kind and understanding Americans. Likewise, the Americans found the Japanese people cooperative and polite. Although they were meeting under awkward conditions, both sides were remarkably calm.

Much credit for this peaceful beginning belongs to two men—the Japanese emperor who announced the surrender to his people, and the American general who accepted the surrender. The Japanese people had seldom seen Emperor Hirohito. Never before had they heard him speak. His radio broadcast had stunned the nation. Until then, the emperor had been worshipped as a god. Soldiers in battle willingly gave up their lives for him. With the war lost, Hirohito gave up his godlike image and went out to mingle with his people for the first time.

MacArthur's official title was supreme commander of Allied forces in the Pacific. In Japan and in the United States, he, his position, and his headquarters were all simply referred to as SCAP.

Although very little happened in Japan without SCAP approval, MacArthur's orders were to be carried out by the Japanese themselves. SCAP's General Order Number One, for example, allowed Japanese soldiers to turn in their own weapons. MacArthur knew that if American troops took the rifles and swords from the Japanese by force, the Japanese would feel shame that might later lead to unnecessary trouble.

American advisers urged MacArthur to order the emperor to appear before him. Many Americans wanted to do away with the position of emperor. Some even wanted Hirohito brought to trial as a war criminal. MacArthur did not approve these ideas. First, Douglas understood the importance of the emperor to Japanese life—embarrassing Hirohito would serve only to arouse a Japanese public still numbed by the shock of defeat. Second, MacArthur knew that his own rule over Japan could not succeed without the cooperation of the emperor.

On September 27, the emperor of Japan requested an appointment with the supreme commander. The meeting took place at the American embassy. Later, as MacArthur began describing the details of the emperor's visit, Jean interrupted him with a smile and said, "Oh, I saw him. Arthur and I were peeking behind the red curtains."

Both leaders developed a sincere, if distant, respect for one another. Each Christmas the emperor sent a gift to MacArthur, and the two met at the embassy at least twice a year. However, MacArthur did not often leave Tokyo during his stay in Japan. He ruled, as had the emperor, from a distance. He understood that he was popular among the Japanese because of this cool and grand manner.

On a rare plane trip to Korea, he lit up a corncob pipe. Someone remarked, "Haven't seen you smoke that pipe, General, for years!"

MacArthur nodded and explained, "I don't dare smoke it back there in Tokyo. They'd think I was nothing but a farmer."

General MacArthur seldom met with occupation officials who were not among his closest advisers. The staff who had surrounded him throughout the war kept leadership positions during the occupation, and they were responsible for carrying out SCAP's many orders. The general did, however, meet frequently with visiting journalists and politicians.

*The famous photograph of General MacArthur and the Emperor Hirohito, which was widely published in Japan.*

His schedule was nearly the same each day. Arriving at SCAP headquarters at about half-past ten each morning, he attended to official duties until about half-past one. He then followed the same route back to the embassy. He had lunch, at times entertained important guests, and took a nap. At about four o'clock, he drove back to his office, where he remained until about eight. Day in and day out, seven days a week, he kept to the same schedule.

MacArthur seemed to thrive on his work. He never took a vacation, but he did escape to his home. There, in the roomy embassy, he found time to play with his son or share a quiet moment with his wife. Jean, in turn, supported her husband, whom she affectionately called General or Sir Boss.

To relax, Douglas liked nothing more than to sit in a comfortable chair with a good book from his library or watch one of the films shown nightly in the drawing room. All staff members had a permanent invitation to join the general at the movies. For many, the home-style desserts Jean offered were reward enough for sitting through a sometimes dull film.

During the first year of the occupation, the SCAP organization grew quickly as a new staff of American experts from many fields arrived in Ja-

*Crowds of curious Japanese and Americans gather at the Dai Ichi building to catch a glimpse of Japan's best-known personality.*

pan. Their job seemed impossible—to transform a centuries-old society into a modern democracy.

First, SCAP had to bring home millions of U.S. soldiers and civilians scattered throughout the Pacific. SCAP also had to locate more than one hundred thousand American and Allied soldiers who were still in Japanese prisoner-of-war camps and to arrange for their release.

Next, the Japanese accused of war crimes were brought to trial. Many of the top military leaders were found guilty. Some—like General Homma who was in charge of the Philippines during the

Bataan Death March—were sentenced to death. Others received long prison terms. Still others, who had played minor roles, were purged (not allowed to hold public office for life).

Finally, SCAP focused on the Japanese people themselves. MacArthur had unusual power to rule, and few in Washington dared question him. Seeing that Japanese food supplies were short, he ordered American troops to eat canned rations. He then quickly arranged to import food from the United States to help feed the Japanese people.

SCAP also modernized the Japanese school system, and it took steps to distribute the country's wealth equally. Before the war, well-known families like the Mitsubishis and Sumitomos had controlled most of Japan's industry. The Zaibatsu—as these great industrial giants were known—were broken up. Japanese workers were given the freedom to establish their own labor unions. New land-reform laws allowed peasants to own the land they lived and worked on.

Change did not come overnight. In 1946, Bill Riley, a seventeen-year-old U.S. soldier just assigned to MacArthur's special Honor Guard, traveled by train from Yokohama to Tokyo. He saw ruin and poverty everywhere. Only chimneys stood where houses had once been. Whole families lived in crowded wooden crates that had at one time held airplane parts.

He also saw how kind American soldiers were to the Japanese, especially the children. Japan was soon caught up in an American craze. Anything American was popular. American music played everywhere, and American hairstyles and clothes became the rage. But these influences were only skin-deep.

MacArthur wanted a true Japanese democracy that went beyond the surface. He set out to create a new constitution for Japan, which SCAP officials developed. MacArthur insisted that the new constitution contain three major points: first, Japan must never again go to war; second, Japan's feudal system, with its wealthy landlords and poor tenants, must be ended; and third, all reforms must be accomplished while keeping the office of the emperor.

When the Diet (the Japanese parliament) adopted the new constitution in 1947, Japan's social and political life was forever changed. The emperor became only the symbol of the Japanese nation and was no longer considered a god. Women, who in the past had been treated as second-class citizens, were now equal to men, with full legal and voting rights. All citizens gained the right to equal justice in the courts. Finally, to make sure that the new Japan would never be a threat to peace, Article IX of the constitution clearly forbid Japan to have an army or navy.

Public relations was an important part of the SCAP organization. Both in Japan and the United States, news about the occupation and MacArthur streamed forth. The news was usually good—so good that by the presidential election of 1948, General MacArthur was mentioned as a Republican candidate.

MacArthur did nothing to silence that kind of talk; rather, he encouraged it. However, it would have been difficult for him to campaign across the Pacific, and he had no intention of going home to America, even for a visit.

On August 15, 1948, MacArthur visited Seoul, the capital of South Korea, to see Syngman Rhee sworn in as that nation's first president. At the time, MacArthur did not realize what an effect Korea would soon have on his career.

# Chapter/Ten

## *War in Korea*

On June 25, 1950, North Korea declared war on South Korea. Well-trained North Korean troops crossed the Thirty-eighth Parallel under cover of heavy shelling. The attack shocked and surprised the U.S. government. MacArthur decided that South Korea's army was near collapse and could not protect its capital of Seoul.

From 1910 to 1945, Korea had been a territory of Japan. At the end of World War II, the United States and the Soviet Union had divided Korea into two areas. The Soviet Union was responsible for North Korea, and the United States was responsible for South Korea. The border between North and South Korea was chosen by army officers who found that the country divided neatly at

# Korea: 1950-1953

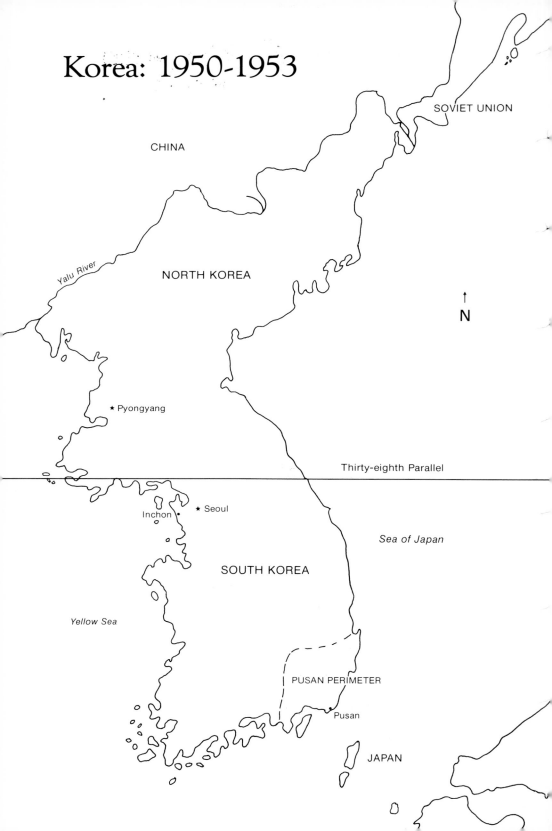

SOVIET UNION

CHINA

Yalu River

NORTH KOREA

N

★ Pyongyang

Thirty-eighth Parallel

Inchon ★ Seoul

Sea of Japan

SOUTH KOREA

Yellow Sea

PUSAN PERIMETER

Pusan

JAPAN

the Thirty-eighth Parallel line printed on the map. That imaginary line through the Korean countryside soon became the best-known geographic landmark in the world. It also caused Douglas MacArthur many sleepless nights.

The United States government was afraid the Korean War would spread into the Soviet Union and Communist China. But Truman also thought that if the United States did not respond, the Soviet Union would believe it could overrun any weak country it wished, in Asia or in Europe. The president turned to the United Nations for support. The United States did not wish to enter Korea without international cooperation. It was hoped that this united effort would discourage the Communists from a larger war.

The United Nations organized a command of troops from seventeen countries. The United States was put in charge, and President Truman appointed seventy-year-old Douglas MacArthur as commander in chief of United Nations forces. MacArthur sent a message thanking him for his confidence, which ended, "I hope I will not fail you."

At first, MacArthur did not have much to work with—only four army divisions were scattered through Japan. He gathered a small force together and sent it to Korea. His goal was to hold and protect South Korea's port of Pusan as a safe entrance for future troops and supplies. Already, North Koreans were in Seoul and had overrun nearly all the south except the Pusan Perimeter, a small, heavily guarded land area in the southeast corner of Korea.

When MacArthur flew to South Korea for a firsthand look, what he saw did not please him. The South Korean forces lacked organization as well as heavy guns. The roads were crowded with refugees fleeing the advancing Communist armies. MacArthur informed the Joint Chiefs of Staff that he needed more troops immediately. "Unless provision is made for the full utilization of the Army-Navy-Air team in this shattered area, our mission will be needlessly costly in life, money, and prestige. At worst, it might even be doomed to failure."

MacArthur received permission to increase American military forces. Truman was concerned about widening the war. He ordered the U.S. Seventh Fleet to the China Sea to make sure there would be no fighting between Chiang Kai-shek and Communist China.

Chiang Kai-shek was a Chinese general who had fled Communist mainland China and established a non-Communist base on the island of Formosa. MacArthur believed that Chiang Kai-shek

In 1951, MacArthur (in the front passenger seat) *visits the Korean front in his official jeep with the five-star general license plate.*

could play a key military role in support of the Americans in Asia. President Truman, however, did not trust Chiang Kai-shek and had given MacArthur a direct order not to accept any offer of Chinese troops.

When the Chinese leader did offer his troops to the United States, MacArthur was interested, and traveled to Formosa to meet with him. Truman was annoyed that MacArthur had even taken the trip to Formosa.

In August, MacArthur found himself in the midst of a public relations problem. The Korean War was on the minds of Americans as news spread of fierce battles and American losses. The Veterans of Foreign Wars (VFW) asked MacArthur to send a message about the war to their convention. MacArthur responded by criticizing U.S. foreign policy and stating his position that Formosa was the key to operations in the Pacific.

The contents of MacArthur's message were leaked to the press two days before the convention. President Truman was angry. The Secretary of Defense sent MacArthur a top-secret personal telegram: "The President of the United States directs that you withdraw your message for National Encampment of Veterans of Foreign Wars, because various features with respect to Formosa are in conflict with the Policy of the United States and its position in the United Nations."

It was MacArthur's turn to be angry. He answered with a defense of his actions: "My remarks were calculated solely to support . . . and I am unable to see wherein they might be interpreted otherwise. The views were purely my personal ones." He asked President Truman to reconsider the order. He then closed with a request to forward this statement to the VFW commander at the Sherman Hotel in Chicago: "I regret to inform you that I have been directed to withdraw my message." But the damage had been done. The split between President Truman and General MacArthur was now public knowledge.

As United Nations troops began arriving in force, North Korean attacks against Pusan grew weaker. By mid-September, the Allies were ready to regain control of South Korea. The only question was how.

MacArthur had thought about the answer to that question for a long time. His hope was to cut off the North Korean supply route and begin attacks from the north. At the same time, Allied troops would break out of the Pusan area. North Korean troops would be cut off and thrown back across the Thirty-eighth Parallel.

Drawing upon World War II successes with sea-based landings, MacArthur proposed a daring plan to surprise the North Koreans. He would land troops behind enemy lines at Inchon, only twenty-five miles from Seoul. Inchon seemed a most unlikely place for an invasion; the approach to the harbor was dangerous and could only be attempted at high tide.

Experts determined that for the upcoming month, the only date on which a landing could take place was September 15. The entrance to the port was guarded by the island of Wolmi-do and a high seawall that faced the port. MacArthur informed the Joint Chiefs that the plan "represents the only hope of wresting the initiative from the enemy . . . . To do otherwise is to commit us to a war of indefinite duration."

On September 12, MacArthur boarded the *Mount McKinley* and joined the invasion fleet of two hundred ships headed toward Inchon. On the morning of September 15, the marines landed at Wolmi-do.

MacArthur's plan proved brilliant. The American troops caught the enemy off guard and landed successfully. By the end of the month, they had pushed most North Korean soldiers back across the border.

On September 29, MacArthur and South Korea's president, Syngman Rhee, held a brief but
moving ceremony in Seoul. The government of
South Korea was back in its own capital. MacArthur received congratulations from many world
leaders. President Truman cabled, "Well and nobly
done!"

At first, the United Nations did not allow Mac-
Arthur to cross the Thirty-eighth Parallel border
into North Korean territory. But on October 7, the
United Nations finally gave MacArthur permission
to cross the border and unify North and South
Korea into a single country. By mid-October, U.N.
troops were well inside North Korea approaching
the Chinese border. There was talk that American
troops would be home by Thanksgiving.

President Truman still had questions about the
intentions of the Chinese and the Soviets. He called
MacArthur to a face-to-face meeting on October
15. Truman did not trust MacArthur. He did not
like him, either. Several years earlier, in his diary,
the president had called the general, "Mr. Prima
Donna, Brass Hat, Five-Star MacArthur." Now, on
the plane ride to the meeting, he referred to the
general as "God's right-hand man."

The two men met on Wake Island, halfway
between Japan and Hawaii, to make decisions on

*Despite the difficulties between Truman and MacArthur, they remained cordial to one another. On Wake Island, October 1950, President Truman awards MacArthur another Distinguished Service Medal.*

the future role of the United Nations in Korea. When asked what chance there was of China's entering the war, MacArthur told the president, "Very little . . . we are no longer fearful of their intervention." If the Chinese involved themselves militarily, MacArthur added, they would face "the greatest slaughter."

Shortly after this meeting, the United Nations troops faced stiff fighting as they approached the Manchurian border. MacArthur was not overly concerned. He did not realize that the Chinese were busily putting together a 300,000-man army. Mac-

Arthur thought the war in Korea was over, but it was only beginning.

On November 7, MacArthur sent a flash bulletin to Washington: "Men and material in large force are pouring across all bridges over the Yalu from Manchuria." Since MacArthur's orders specifically said he could not attack Chinese positions beyond the Yalu River, he requested permission to destroy the bridges. But Washington was careful. The Joint Chiefs of Staff would not let MacArthur attack Chinese territory, but they finally allowed him to bomb the Yalu bridges on the South Korean side.

"We face an entirely new war," MacArthur reported to Washington. United Nations troops could not stand up to the huge Chinese forces, and they retreated southward. MacArthur was angry. He again asked Washington to allow him to bomb Communist bases in Manchuria across the Yalu River. He asked to use Chiang Kai-shek's troops from Formosa against the North Koreans and Communist Chinese.

Again, MacArthur's requests were denied. American leaders were afraid the conflict would widen into a third world war.

The Joint Chiefs of Staff began preparations for removing American troops from Korea if conditions grew worse. "We believe," they explained to MacArthur, "that Korea is not the place to fight a major war." As MacArthur understood it, the United States no longer thought it could win in Korea. He made his displeasure known in remarks to journalists and in letters to influential contacts in America. MacArthur believed that if the United States failed to win the war in Korea, the world—particularly the Soviet Union—would view America as a weak and spineless country.

On December 6, President Truman ordered all army commanders to submit any future press releases, statements, and speeches to Washington for approval. No one doubted that this order was directed at one specific officer—General of the Army MacArthur.

Truman understood MacArthur's anger, however. On January 13, 1951, he sent the general a telegram outlining the government's position in Korea. Its goal was to make possible a satisfactory peace settlement. The president said he recognized that the actions of U.S. forces in Korea were being limited, but that these troops had to be saved in case Japan was attacked. "In reaching a final decision about Korea," Truman added, "I shall have to give constant thought to the main threat from the Soviet Union."

MacArthur responded to the president immediately: "We shall do our best."

By then, however, Communist troops had thrown U.N. troops southward over the Thirty-eighth Parallel. Seoul again fell to the Communists. In a series of savage advances, the Americans slowly turned the tide of battle and pushed the fighting back to the old border at the Thirty-eighth Parallel. MacArthur asked Washington to take more direct action against the Chinese. After visiting Korea in early March, he issued a statement: "Vital decisions have yet to be made—decisions far beyond the scope of the authority vested in me as the Military Commander."

On March 15, U.N. forces again reentered Seoul—this time for good. As fighting along the border grew heavier, some of the bloodiest battles of the war took place. On barren hills with names like Heartbreak Ridge, Bloody Ridge, and Pork Chop Hill, young soldiers gave their lives to prevent further loss of territory. Their bravery again freed South Korea from its Communist invaders.

The United Nations hoped the Chinese would agree to a cease-fire (an end to the fighting) that would lead to a settlement. In late March, MacArthur was informed in a top-secret message that President Truman was about to issue an important an-

nouncement concerning peace talks. A few days
after receiving that message, MacArthur issued a
harsh public statement in which he demanded the
surrender of Chinese forces. President Truman was
enraged. MacArthur had destroyed any chance for
peace, and Truman's planned announcement would
not be released.

In the same month, MacArthur wrote to Congressman Joseph W. Martin, Jr., of Massachusetts.
Martin favored bringing General Chiang Kai-shek's
troops into the war. MacArthur wrote: "If we lose
this war to Communism in Asia, the fall of Europe
is inevitable. . .as you point out, we must win.
There is no substitute for victory." Congressman
Martin made MacArthur's letter public.

Truman viewed MacArthur's actions as openly
against the president and the Constitution of the
United States. Article II, Section 2, of the Constitution declares, "The President shall be Commander-in-Chief of the Army and Navy of the United
States." This control of the military is a basic principle of American democracy. In President Truman's eyes, MacArthur had broken that principle.

On April 11, 1951, MacArthur received a message from President Truman: "I deeply regret that it
becomes my duty as President and Commander-in-
Chief of the United States Military Forces to re-

place you as Supreme Commander, Allied Powers; Commander-in-Chief, United Nations Command; Commander-in-Chief, Far East; and Commanding General, U.S. Army, Far East."

Upon hearing the news, MacArthur turned to his wife and said, simply, "Jeannie, we're going home at last."

The Japanese were losing a respected leader—the man who had taken them from defeat to democracy. An article in the *Nippon Times* summarized their feelings: "The Japanese people owe General MacArthur an eternal debt of gratitude."

Emperor Hirohito requested a farewell audience with MacArthur. With tears in his eyes, the emperor clutched MacArthur's hands.

On April 16, 200,000 Japanese citizens lined the roads to Atsugi airport as MacArthur began his journey home. The *Bataan* took off to the sounds of a nineteen-gun salute and a military band playing "Auld Lang Syne."

# Chapter/Eleven

## *Home at Last*

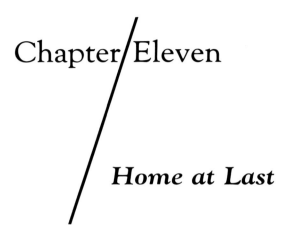

The MacArthurs' homecoming was the beginning of a series of firsts. It was the first time Douglas and Jean had been back in the United States since 1937 when they married. It was also the first time thirteen-year-old Arthur had set foot in his own country.

From the moment their plane landed at Hickam Air Force Base in Hawaii on April 16, 1951, the MacArthurs were mobbed by wave after wave of adoring crowds. Hawaii, which had felt the first Japanese blow with the attack on Pearl Harbor, greeted MacArthur and his family royally. One hundred thousand people lined the parade route as the general passed by.

Two days later was MacArthur Day in San

Francisco. When he saw the city from the air, Mac-Arthur put an arm over his son's shoulder and said, "Well, my boy, we're home." Their arrival was marked by another parade and an official welcome at city hall. As he addressed the cheering crowd, a "MacArthur for President" sign waved in the background. The general turned aside such political plans—at least in public—by saying, "No . . . I have no political aspirations . . . the only politics I have is contained in the simple phrase known well by all of you: God bless America."

From San Francisco it was on to the East. In Washington, D.C., MacArthur was welcomed as a national hero; schools were closed and government workers were given half a day off. MacArthur was invited to address a joint session of Congress, an honor normally given to the U.S. president and heads of foreign governments.

On April 19, MacArthur delivered a speech that was broadcast to the nation live over radio and television. He spoke of America's involvement in Korea and justified his own views: "Once war is forced upon us, there is no other alternative than to apply every available means to bring it to a swift end. War's very object is victory—not prolonged indecision. In war, indeed, there can be no substitute for victory."

Then he added, "I have just left your fighting
sons in Korea. They have met all tests there and...
they are splendid in every way. Those gallant men
will remain often in my thoughts and in my prayers
always."

He ended his speech with these words:

> I am closing my fifty-two years of military service.
> When I joined the Army even before the turn of
> the century, it was the fulfillment of all my boyish
> hopes and dreams. The world has turned over
> many times since I took the oath on the plain at
> West Point, and the hopes and dreams have long
> since vanished. But I still remember the refrain of
> one of the most popular barrack ballads of that
> day which proclaimed most proudly that—"Old
> soldiers never die; they just fade away." And like
> the old soldier of that ballad, I now close my
> military career and just fade away—an old soldier
> who tried to do his duty as God gave him the light
> to see that duty. Goodbye.

Leaving the Capitol, the general rode in a
twenty-car motorcade down Pennsylvania Avenue.
As the parade passed the hundreds of thousands
of flag-waving people who lined the sidewalks,
military jets flew overhead. When the motorcade
arrived at the Washington Monument, cannons
boomed a thunderous seventeen-gun salute.

But none of this could match the outpouring of sincere affection that greeted MacArthur in New York. After spending the night in the Waldorf Astoria Hotel, the general emerged to the greatest welcome ever given by New York City. Seven million onlookers mobbed the streets to catch a glimpse of MacArthur and his family. The crowds were so thick that it took nearly seven hours to cover the parade route. As the motorcade made its way through Manhattan, office workers tossed an estimated three tons of torn paper out of windows. In the harbor, tugboats and ships added their whistles and horns to the festive din.

All of this might have seemed the natural tribute due a true American hero, had it not been for the simple fact that MacArthur had been dismissed from his position by the president of the United States.

In May 1951, a U.S. Senate Committee opened hearings on the dismissal. For forty days, the committee listened to speaker after speaker explain the U.S. role in Korea. General MacArthur appeared for three full days. After a while, the hearings lost the interest of the American people.

In Korea, the fighting continued as truce talks stretched on and on. Lieutenant General Matthew Ridgway, MacArthur's replacement in the Far

East, suggested a meeting between Allied and Communist military forces on June 30. The truce talks were stalled for months over the prisoner-of-war issue. The United Nations believed that prisoners should be allowed to choose whether or not they wanted to return to their homelands. The Communist forces disagreed.

Finally, in July 1953, the United Nations forces and the Communist forces signed an armistice agreement. Korea was divided at the Thirty-eighth Parallel, separated by a buffer zone. North and South Korea agreed not to increase their military strength, but the two countries never unified, and never reached a final peace settlement.

Although Douglas MacArthur was no longer in the military, he did not "just fade away." The general, Jean, and Arthur (along with Ah Cheu) settled into an elegant ten-room suite on the thirty-seventh floor of the Waldorf Astoria in New York. Arthur enrolled in school and became familiar with the American way of life. Jean began to enjoy the culture and shops of New York City. Douglas kept up a busy schedule of speeches, meetings, and public appearances throughout the country. Parks were named after him, state legislatures welcomed him, and he was presented with honorary degrees.

On September 8, 1951, Japan and its former

*Douglas, Jean, and Arthur wave to the welcoming crowds in 1951.*

enemies signed their formal peace treaty in San
Francisco. Among those not present—he was not
invited—was MacArthur, the man who had made
it possible for Japan to be counted among the free
nations. Some thought this was President Truman's
final revenge.

In 1952, MacArthur became chairman of the
board of Remington Rand Corporation. His job
allowed time for speaking and attending to his
many interests—including Republican politics.
MacArthur considered running for the Republican
nomination in the 1952 presidential election, but
he did not. He ended up delivering the keynote
speech at the Republican National Convention in
Chicago. MacArthur's former aide, General Dwight
Eisenhower, was selected as the Republican presidential candidate.

The years after 1952 were quiet ones for the
MacArthurs. They enjoyed Broadway theater together and the general frequently attended prize
fights and baseball games.

From time to time MacArthur met with old
army comrades to tell combat stories. One of his
Waldorf Astoria neighbors was former president
Herbert Hoover. The old friends frequently dis-
cussed events past and present.

Although Truman had taken away his com-

*MacArthur looks on proudly as his son tries on a West Point cadet hat.*

mands, MacArthur would hold his five-star General of the Army rank for life. In 1959, he became the highest-ranking officer in the U.S. Army.

Each year, MacArthur looked forward to meeting a new group of West Point cadets. The general hoped his son would follow in his footsteps.

One of young Arthur's first stops in the United States was West Point. There he tried on the traditional cadet shako (hat). When the time came for Arthur to go to college, however, Arthur chose Columbia University, not West Point. His father may have been disappointed, but he did not show it. When Arthur graduated from Columbia in 1961, both proud parents were in the audience.

The following year, Douglas MacArthur, Class of 1903, was invited to West Point to receive the academy's highest honor, the Thayer Award. There he delivered what many consider his finest speech:

> The shadows are lengthening for me. The twilight is here. My days of old have vanished—tone and tint. They have gone glimmering through the dreams of things that were. . . .In my dreams I hear again the crash of guns, the rattle of musketry, the strange mournful mutter of the battlefield. But in the evening of my memory always I come back to West Point. Always there echoes and reechoes: Duty, Honor, Country.
>
> Today marks my final rollcall with you. But I want you to know that, when I cross the river, my last conscious thoughts will be of the corps, and the corps, and the corps. I bid you farewell.

General of the Army Douglas MacArthur died on April 5, 1964, at Walter Reed Army Hospital in Washington. In New York, the West Point band and a large group of cadets led a military funeral parade. His body was then returned to Washington, D.C., where another formal parade led to the Capitol rotunda. There he lay in state until the next day. He was buried in Norfolk, Virginia.

Across the James River from the site of his mother's family estate, Riveredge, is the MacAr-

*The MacArthur Memorial.*

thur Memorial and museum. The beautiful building was once the Norfolk City Hall. In the rotunda, surrounded by the general's own memorable words carved in marble, is MacArthur's crypt. Several flags line the wall around the crypt. Two of these especially represent the man and his career: one is a flag bearing the five stars of a General of the Army; the other is the flag of the United States of America.

# Appendix

## Major Events in MacArthur's Life

1880    Douglas MacArthur is born on January 26

1897    MacArthur graduates from the West Texas Military Academy

1903    MacArthur graduates from West Point and is commissioned a second lieutenant in the United States Army

1912    Captain Douglas MacArthur is appointed to the Army General Staff in Washington, D.C.

1914-18    World War I begins in 1914, and the United States enters the war in 1917; MacArthur promoted to brigadier general in 1918

1919    MacArthur appointed superintendent of West Point

1922    MacArthur marries Louise Cromwell Brooks

1927    Major General MacArthur is named president of the United States Olympic Committee

1929   MacArthur and Louise Brooks are divorced

1930   President Hoover appoints MacArthur as army chief of staff

1934   The Philippine government requests MacArthur's service as military adviser

1937   MacArthur marries Jean Marie Faircloth in New York

1938   MacArthur's only son, Arthur IV, is born on February 21 in Manila

1939-45 World War II begins in 1939, and the United States enters war in 1941; MacArthur escapes from the Philippines to direct the Pacific war against Japan; MacArthur is awarded the Medal of Honor by President Roosevelt; MacArthur becomes General of the Army

1945   The Japanese surrender to MacArthur on September 2; MacArthur becomes supreme commander of the Allied forces in Japan

1950   The Korean War begins; MacArthur disagrees with President Truman's policy

1951   MacArthur is fired by President Truman and returns home as a hero

1964   MacArthur dies on April 5, and is buried in Norfolk, Virginia

# Selected Bibliography

Ambrose, Stephen. *Eisenhower, Soldier, General of the Army, President-Elect 1890-1952.* New York: Simon & Schuster, 1983.

Blair, Clay, Jr. *MacArthur.* Garden City: Doubleday, 1977.

Hunt, Frazier. *The Untold Story of Douglas MacArthur.* New York: Devin-Adair, 1954.

James, D. Clayton. *The Years of MacArthur.* (3 Volumes), Boston: Houghton Mifflin, 1970-85.

MacArthur, Douglas. *Reminiscences.* New York: McGraw-Hill, 1964.

"MacArthur Hearing: Debate With Destiny." *Time* (May 14, 1951), 19-25.

"MacArthur Hearing." *Time* (June 25, 1951), 18.

"MacArthur v. Truman." *Time* (April 23, 1951), 31-32.

Manchester, William. *American Caesar.* Boston: Little, Brown, 1978.

Marrin, Albert. *Victory in the Pacific.* New York: Atheneum, 1983.

———. *The Yanks Are Coming.* New York: Atheneum, 1986.

Marshall, S.L.A. *The Military History of the Korean War.* New York: Watts, 1963.

Middleton, Harry. *The Compact History of the Korean War.* New York: Hawthorn, 1965.

Raymond, Jack. "MacArthur Is Dead; Led Allied Force in Japan's Defeat." *New York Times* (April 6, 1964), 1.

*Representative Speeches of General of the Army Douglas MacArthur.* Washington: U.S. Government Printing Office, 1964.

Rosenthal, A.M. "Truman Relieves MacArthur." *New York Times* (May 11, 1951), 1.

Rovere, Richard. *The General and the President.* New York: Farrar, Straus and Young, 1951.

Spector, Ronald. *Eagle Against the Sun.* New York: Free Press, 1984.

Stallings, Lawrence. *The Doughboys: The Story of the AEF.* New York: Harper & Row, 1963.

Truman, Harry S. *Years of Trial and Hope 1946-1952.* Garden City: Doubleday, 1956.

# / Index

128

superintendent of West Point, 38-40, 44; as supreme commander of Allied forces in the Pacific (SCAP), 6, 83-86, 87-96; as supreme commander of United Nations forces, 99-111. Poem: "Build Me a Son," 57-59

MacArthur, Jean (second wife), 54, 55, 56-57, 64, 67, 75, 80, 90, 92, 111, 112, 116, 118, 119

MacArthur, Louise (first wife), 40-41, 42, 44, 45

MacArthur, Malcolm (brother), 7, 10

MacArthur, Mary "Pinky" (mother), 7, 8-11, 13, 14-16, 17, 19-20, 22-23, 25, 26-27, 33, 40, 41, 42, 46, 54, 56, 120

MacArthur Memorial, 120-121

Malinta Tunnel, 64

Martin, Joseph W., Jr., 110

Medal of Honor, 6, 7, 28, 36, 37, 69

National Guard, 29-30

New Deal, 52

Nimitz, Chester, 70

Olympics, 44-45

Osmena, Sergio, 77

Otjen, Theabold, 14, 16

Pershing, John, 37, 42

Potsdam Declaration, 81-82

Quezon, Manual, 22, 45-46, 53-54, 56, 61, 64, 66, 77

Rainbow Division, 30-33, 34, 36. See also Forty-second Division

Ridgway, Matthew, 115-116

Riley, Bill, 94-95

Roosevelt, Franklin D., 51-52, 53, 54, 60, 66, 67, 68, 69, 76, 79, 81

Roosevelt, Theodore, 25

Russo-Japanese War, 22

SCAP, 89, 90, 92-94, 95, 96

Spanish-American War, 16-17, 21

Summerall, Charles, 36, 44

Syngman Rhee, 96, 105

Thirty-eighth Parallel, 97-99, 103, 105, 109, 116

Truman, Harry S., 81, 82, 83, 87-88, 99, 100, 102-103, 105-106, 108, 109-111, 118-119

United Nations, 99, 103, 105-106, 107, 109, 116

U.S. Forest Service, 52

U.S. Military Academy at West Point, 14, 16, 17, 18-19, 20, 38-40, 44, 119, 120

V-J (Victory over Japan) Day, 82-83

Veterans of Foreign Wars (VFW), 102-103

Wainwright, Jonathan, 67, 85, 86

West Side High School, 16

West Texas Military Academy, 13, 16, 26

Wilson, Woodrow, 27, 29, 30

Wood, Leonard, 27

World War I, 29, 31-37, 38, 49

World War II, 6, 61-69, 70-83, 97, 104